A SOLDIER'S LIFE IN

WORLD WAR TWO

A SOLDIER'S LIFE IN

WORLD WAR TWO

Fiona Corbridge

FRANKLIN WATTS
LONDON•SYDNEY

Illustrations by:
Mark Bergin
Kevin Maddison
Lee Montgomery
Peter Visscher
Mike White
Maps by Stefan Chabluk

First published in 2006 by
Franklin Watts
338 Euston Road
London NW1 3BH

Franklin Watts Australia
Hachette Children's Books
Level 17/207 Kent Street
Sydney NSW 2000

Series editor: John C. Miles
Art director: Jonathan Hair

This book is based on
Going to War in World War One
by Moira Butterfield © Franklin Watts 2000
It is produced for Franklin Watts
by Painted Fish Ltd.
Designer: Rita Storey

A CIP catalogue record
for this book is available
from the British Library

ISBN 0 7496 6496 7

Dewey classification: 355.0094'054

Printed in China

CONTENTS

HOW WAR STARTED

In 1918, Germany lost World War One. It had to give up land and was banned from having armed forces.

Adolf Hitler led a political party in Germany called the National Socialists, or Nazis. He got into power in 1933. The Nazis quickly began to arm Germany again and to seize land from other countries. This led to World War Two (the Second World War), which lasted from 1939 to 1945.

CANADA

USA

Battle of the Atlantic 1939–45

ATLANTIC OCEAN

The two sides in World War Two

- **The Axis powers**
Germany, with Italy and Japan.

- **The Allies**
Britain and other countries. Later joined by the USSR and the USA.

1939
Germany invades Poland. War is declared by Britain, France, Australia, New Zealand and Canada.

German leader Adolf Hitler

1940
German troops conquer most of France. Italy enters the war. Germans bomb British cities in the Blitz.

British Prime Minister Winston Churchill

1941
Germans go into North Africa and the USSR. Japan attacks the USA and it joins the war.

US President Franklin Roosevelt

NORWAY

GREAT
BRITAIN

SWEDEN

FINLAND

*Eastern Front
1941–45*

*War in Europe
1939–45*

PORTUGAL

SPAIN

TURKEY

UNION OF SOVIET SOCIALIST REPUBLICS
(USSR)

*African
campaigns
1939–43*

EGYPT

CHINA

INDIA

BURMA

SOUTH-EAST ASIA

MANCHURIA

JAPAN

*War in the Pacific
and Far East 1940–45*

PHILIPPINES

PACIFIC OCEAN

INDIAN OCEAN

AUSTRALIA

NEW ZEALAND

WORLD
MAP 1942

Allied powers

Axis powers

Countries occupied
by the Axis powers

Neutral European
countries

*Major areas
of fighting*

1942
Germans
stopped in
USSR. Allies
fight Japan
with success
and win in
North Africa.

**Russian
dictator
Joseph
Stalin**

1943
Mussolini
loses
power in
Italy. Allies
invade Italy
and bomb
German cities.

**Italian
dictator
Benito
Mussolini**

1944
Allies drive
Germans
back in Italy
and invade
France. USA
starts beating
Japan.

1945
Allies
advance.
Hitler dies.
Germany
surrenders.
Nuclear bombs force
Japan to surrender.

**Japanese
Emperor
Hirohito**

BLITZKRIEG!

On 1 September 1939, Germany attacked Poland. The Germans used a new way of fighting called blitzkrieg, meaning "lightning war".

During 1939 and 1940, German forces spread across Europe. They invaded France, the Netherlands, Norway, Denmark, Luxembourg and Belgium. These countries were now occupied, or under German control.

NETHERLANDS, BELGIUM AND FRANCE 1939–40

← Main route of German attack
← Other German attacks

BRITAIN
NETHERLANDS
Amsterdam
Dunkirk
BELGIUM
Brussels
GERMANY
Paris
FRANCE

FAST FIGHTING

In the blitzkrieg, the Germans attacked quickly. They used different tactics at the same time. Aircraft bombed targets such as railway lines. Ground forces, including tanks, surrounded enemy armies and forced them to surrender.

HITLER AND THE NAZIS

Hitler was a dictator. He made everyone do what he said and got rid of anyone who disagreed with him.

The Nazis were strict and all Germans had to obey their rules. They also thought that Germany should rule over other countries.

A German tank in the blitzkrieg invasion

Swastika
This was the symbol of the Nazi party. It was a cross with the ends of the arms bent clockwise.

DISASTER AT DUNKIRK

When Germany invaded France, Britain sent a large army there. But in June 1940 it had to retreat (move back) to the coast at Dunkirk. Britain needed lots of ships to rescue the troops. Destroyers, ferries and other boats took part. German aeroplanes attacked during the rescue and killed many soldiers.

Long lines of troops wait to be rescued from the beaches at Dunkirk

A British recruit dresses in his uniform

THE CALL-UP

In 1940, two million British men aged 19–27 years were ordered to fight. This was known as being "called up". They were trained and sent off to war.

GERMAN FORCES

Wehrmacht
German armed forces were called the *Wehrmacht*.

Luftwaffe
The German air force was called the *Luftwaffe*. It was very powerful.

The SS
The SS was a separate army of ruthless military police. They ruled in the occupied countries.

BATTLE IN THE SKY

Hitler planned to invade Britain. To make this easier, he sent the *Luftwaffe* to destroy Britain's Royal Air Force (RAF) first. The RAF and the *Luftwaffe* fought each other in the Battle of Britain. The RAF managed to win.

Just afterwards, Hitler started to bomb British cities heavily. This campaign was known as the Blitz.

London on fire during the Blitz

THE BLITZ
Between 1940–41 the *Luftwaffe* bombed many British cities every night. Thousands of people were killed or injured in these air raids.

AIR RAID ALERT!
When enemy bombers were on the way, wailing sirens warned everyone. People rushed to hide in underground air-raid shelters until they heard an "all-clear" siren.

London Underground stations were used as shelters

RADAR

Britain had a good radar system. It was used to find out when enemy aircraft were on the way. It was a big help in the Battle of Britain.

Bombs
• *High explosives were dropped to blow up buildings.*
• *Fire bombs called incendiaries started fires that spread fast.*

RAF LIFE

At RAF bases, pilots waited until they heard that enemy aircraft were heading for Britain. Then they ran to their planes to take off and fight them in the air.

Crews on the ground kept in radio contact with the pilots and passed on information to help them.

An RAF fighter pilot in flying kit. He had a helmet and a parachute

British Hurricanes and Spitfires attack a German Junkers Ju-88

THE BATTLE OF BRITAIN

The *Luftwaffe* tried to destroy the RAF. Their campaign became known as the Battle of Britain.

Single-seater fighter aeroplanes fought each other in the skies over Britain. Both sides lost many men and planes.

But the RAF managed to survive and spoil Hitler's plan to get rid of them. The *Luftwaffe* had to reduce its raids.

NEW BATTLEGROUNDS

Germany and the USSR had agreed not to fight each other. But then Germany started to attack the USSR.

America was not in the war. But then Japanese forces bombed its naval base at Pearl Harbor, Hawaii, entering the war on the German side.

By the end of 1941, the USSR and the USA had joined the Allies to fight the Germans.

Japanese soldier

WAR IN THE SNOW

Germany fought the USSR in an area called the Eastern Front. In winter it was bitterly cold. The USSR's troops were called the Red Army. They wore warm, white suits that camouflaged (hid) them in the snow.

Both sides had huge losses of men and equipment during 1941–42.

A Russian Red Army soldier in a snow suit

JAPAN

Japan began invading other countries in the 1930s. It planned to conquer India and Australia and create a giant new empire with the Nazis.

The front
When soldiers went to "the front", it meant the area where the armies were fighting each other. The "front line" meant the troops that had gone forward closest to the enemy.

THE RESISTANCE

Soldiers from many countries fought on the Allied side. Among them were troops from Australia, New Zealand and Canada.

People who lived in the occupied countries hated their new rulers, the Nazis. Some used sabotage to make life difficult for the Nazis. These brave, secret helpers were called resistance fighters. They risked being killed if they were caught.

Canadian (left) and Australian soldiers fought for the Allies

PEARL HARBOR

In 1941, the Japanese made a surprise attack against the USA. Their warplanes bombed the giant US fleet at Pearl Harbor, Hawaii. Ships and planes were destroyed; more than 2,400 people were killed.

America was furious and joined the war against Japan and Germany. The strength of the US forces helped the Allies greatly.

American warships on fire after the attack at Pearl Harbor

WOLFPACKS AND WARSHIPS

During the war, merchant ships carried food and supplies to the people of Britain. The ships crossed the North Atlantic from the USA and Canada. German U-boats (submarines) kept trying to sink the ships. The contest was named the Battle of the Atlantic.

HMS *Belfast*, a Royal Navy battlecruiser

SEA WOLVES

U-boats hunted down the merchant ships in groups nicknamed "wolfpacks". The Germans wanted to weaken the British by stopping them getting the food and supplies that they needed.

Radar

Anti-aircraft guns protected the ship from enemy planes

Bridge

PROTECTING THE CONVOYS

Merchant ships sailed in large groups called convoys. Aircraft, destroyers and other warships kept nearby to protect them from German U-boats. Warships tried to destroy the U-boats by dropping depth charges (bombs that exploded underwater).

Sonar
The Allies' warships had a way of finding out where U-boats were. They used a system called sonar, which used sound to find the U-boats underwater.

WAR AT SEA

Mine danger

Both sides put bombs called mines underwater, to try and blow up the enemy's ships. Some floated on wires, others lay on the sea bed.

Sinking ships

Many warships were sunk. On HMS *Hood*, more than 1,400 men died in 1941. The Germans lost the *Graf Spee* in 1939 (right), and the *Bismarck* in 1941.

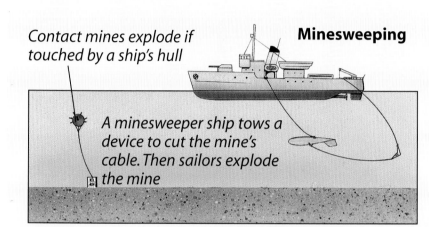

Codebreakers

The Germans used a secret code called Enigma to send messages. Then the British navy captured a U-boat and found items that helped the British to break the code and work out where U-boats were.

Contact mines explode if touched by a ship's hull

Minesweeping

A minesweeper ship tows a device to cut the mine's cable. Then sailors explode the mine

GERMAN NAVY

The *Kriegsmarine* (German navy) had pocket battleships (small cruisers with heavy guns) and very large ships.

LIFE ON BOARD

Life for sailors was tough and they didn't have much space. Sometimes men on different watches (work shifts) had to take it in turns to sleep in the same bed. Everyone was frightened of an enemy attack.

An Allied convoy

WAR IN THE PACIFIC

America and Japan fought fiercely in the Pacific. The US used aircraft carriers, destroyers, submarines and battleships. Its marines (naval soldiers) attacked Japanese forces on land.

Japan occupied many Pacific islands but US forces battled to drive them out. Japan was led by Emperor Hirohito.

Japanese kamikaze aircraft

KAMIKAZE!

In 1944, the Japanese started using suicide pilots called kamikaze. They flew planes packed with explosives into US ships, killing themselves and many others.

LANDING VEHICLES

The US marines went from ship to shore on special landing vehicles that worked in water and on land. These carried troops and tanks.

US marines land on a beach in the Pacific

Japanese army
The Japanese were fierce fighters and hated to surrender. They were also especially cruel to their prisoners.

GIANTS OF THE SEA

Aircraft carriers were a massive floating airbase as well as a warship. Bomber and fighter aeroplanes could take off from them. The US navy had the most carriers.

THE BATTLE OF MIDWAY

In 1942, the Japanese were winning. But at the Battle of Midway, America destroyed four Japanese aircraft carriers. The Japanese did not know that the US had cracked their secret radio codes and knew where and when to attack them.

A Japanese aeroplane attacks a US aircraft carrier

TOUGH TERRAIN

African deserts
Allied troops fought the Germans and Italians in the deserts of North Africa. Tanks battled against each other and tried to destroy enemy positions.

Jungle war
Allied troops fought the Japanese in the jungles of Burma and India. It was mainly close-up fighting.

Disease danger
Conditions in the jungle were horrible. Troops had to cope with monsoon rains, blood-sucking leeches and malaria, a disease spread by the bites of mosquitoes.

LIFE AT HOME

In Britain, life was hard. Food and other things were rationed or disappeared completely. German bombers made terrifying raids.

The USA was not bombed, but the American people worked hard to make guns, ships and tanks for their men fighting far away.

British soldier of the Home Guard

The Sky's the Limit!

KEEP BUYING WAR BONDS

HOME GUARD
Some British men could not join the forces and they helped by joining the Home Guard instead. They learned how to fight in case the enemy arrived in Britain.

THE HOME FRONT
Britain was called the "Home Front", because people felt that they were part of the war. Bombing raids destroyed homes and killed many people.

People bought war bonds to help the government pay for the war

WOMEN IN WARTIME

Women played a vital part in the war. They took over the jobs of men who had gone off to fight. They worked in factories and on farms.

Many women joined the forces as nurses. Some did other important jobs, such as codebreaking, or were radio operators.

Farm worker

Factory worker

Nurse

Auxiliary in the forces

The blackout
In Britain, lights were not allowed to show after dark to make it harder for German bombers to spot their targets. Air-raid wardens patrolled the streets to check that nobody broke this rule.

GIs started a new dance craze, the "jitterbug"

RATIONING

In Britain, people were only allowed to buy a set amount of food per week. When they went shopping, they had to take a ration book and get it stamped by the shopkeeper.

AMERICANS IN BRITAIN

In 1942, US troops began to arrive in Britain to train for fighting in Europe.

Ordinary US troops were called GIs (from the words "government issue" that were on their equipment).

CAPTURE AND ESCAPE

Soldiers who were captured by the enemy became prisoners of war (POWs). They were sent to prisons called POW camps. Many POWs tried to escape and get back home. This was a great risk, because if they were caught, they could be killed.

Escaping
The rules of the British forces said that all captured officers should try to escape.

Colditz Castle in Germany

COLDITZ
Colditz Castle was a famous POW prison. Escape from it was meant to be impossible, but many prisoners did so.

BREAKOUT

Planning to escape
Allied POWs secretly managed to make everyday clothes (below), passports and money to help them get home.

Tunnels
Some POWs dug tunnels to escape from prison. The work could take many months because they didn't have proper tools. They used odds and ends to dig.

On the run
Resistance groups hid escaped prisoners and helped them to get back home. If these helpers were caught by the Nazis, they could be shot.

SECRET FIGHTERS

Resistance fighters in occupied countries sabotaged factories, trains and ports.

They kept in touch with Britain with small portable radios. They had to be careful that the Germans didn't pick up the radio signal and find them.

POWs IN THE FAR EAST

The Japanese kept Allied soldiers and civilians in terrible conditions. They were starved and forced to do very hard work.

Some Allied POWs were forced to work in Japanese mines

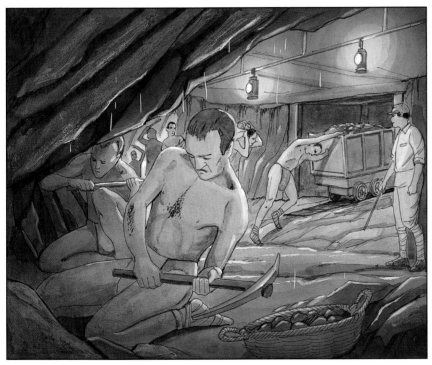

A TERRIBLE SECRET

The Nazis set up prisons called concentration camps. Jews, Gypsies and other peoples were imprisoned there.

Hitler carried out one of the most terrible crimes in history. He had millions of these people killed.

GESTAPO

The Gestapo were the ruthless secret police of the SS. They tortured many captured resistance fighters to make them give information.

A Gestapo officer

HITLER IN TROUBLE

In 1943, things began to go wrong for the Germans. Thousands of German and Italian troops were captured in North Africa. On the Eastern Front in the USSR, Hitler's forces were slowly driven back.

Red Army troops at Stalingrad

Russian T-34 tank

A RUSSIAN VICTORY
In the USSR, the Germans went into the city of Stalingrad. But they were trapped by the Russian Red Army.

The Germans were cut off from supplies and 300,000 men died of cold, starvation, or in the fighting. Their commander disobeyed Hitler and surrendered.

TANK BATTLE
The biggest tank battle in history took place between the German Tiger tanks and Russian T-34 tanks at Kursk in the USSR.

Hundreds of thousands of soldiers died. The Red Army had more than 600,000 casualties (injured people). The German tank forces were badly damaged.

The panzers
Hitler's tank forces were called the panzers. The battle at Kursk became known as the "death ride" of the panzers.

THE ALLIES INVADE ITALY

Beach fighting

Allied troops invaded Sicily on 10 July 1943, and from there landed in Italy. There was fierce gunfire and they were bombed by German aircraft.

Italian surrender

Italy surrendered on 8 September 1943. Most Italian soldiers gave up or changed sides. But the Germans fought hard to hold on to the country.

Monte Cassino in ruins

Battling on

The Germans held the hilltop monastery of Monte Cassino, and blocked the Allies' way to Rome. It took four months of fighting to get rid of them.

BOMBING RAIDS

To try and force the Germans to surrender, the RAF and US Air Force made bombing raids on German cities by day and night.

They also dropped incendiary (fire) bombs to create firestorms that killed thousands.

RAF Lancaster night bomber

US P-51D Mustang fighter

The Mustang had six machine guns in its wings

MUSTANGS

The Mustang was a very good fighter aircraft. It was used to protect US bombers flying to attack Germany.

D-DAY

The Allies had a plan to invade occupied Europe and win it back from the Nazis. They would cross the English Channel and land in northern France. The plan was called Operation Overlord, or D-Day. On 6 June 1944, it began. More than 10,000 planes, 4,000 ships and 156,000 troops took part.

THE D-DAY LANDINGS

Soldiers landed on five beaches codenamed Omaha, Utah, Juno, Sword and Gold. Some parachuted in behind the beaches to take over roads and bridges. Small landing craft took soldiers from large troop ships to the shore. Warships fired at German beach defences.

Steel helmet

Rifle

Belt

First-aid kit

Entrenching tool for digging

Fighting knife

US infantryman

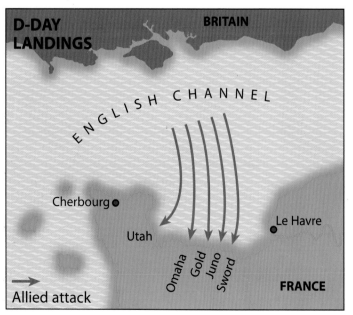

D-DAY LANDINGS

BRITAIN

ENGLISH CHANNEL

Cherbourg

Le Havre

Utah

Omaha
Gold
Juno
Sword

FRANCE

Allied attack

CLEVER INVENTIONS

Some clever new inventions helped the invading Allied armies to land on D-Day.

Floating truck

DUKWs (known as "ducks") could be a boat on water and a truck on land. They carried troops or supplies.

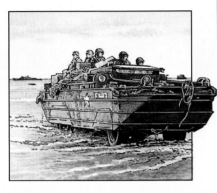

Instant harbours

These were floated across the Channel and then put together. Ships used them to land men and unload supplies.

Weird tanks

Some unusual tanks took part in D-Day: floating tanks, flame-thrower tanks and flail tanks.

The chains on a flail tank beat the ground to explode buried mines

FIGHTING ON THE BEACHES

As the troops landed, the Germans fought back hard.

US troops attacked Omaha beach. It was a difficult job, because the Germans had put mines and underwater traps in the sea for landing craft.

The Americans had to force their way inland to destroy German gun positions. Many Americans were killed.

US troops wade ashore from a landing craft at Omaha beach

THE FINAL PUSH

Allied troops moved inland from the French beaches, fighting the Germans as they went.

The Allies were stronger than the Germans, but commanders disagreed about the best way to fight. This gave the Germans a chance to fight back with a counter-attack (an attack made when an enemy attacks you).

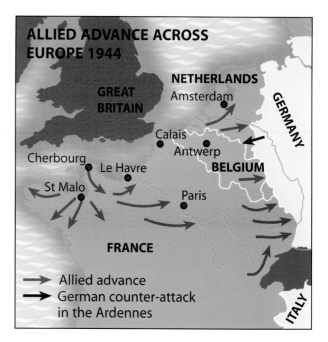

ALLIED ADVANCE ACROSS EUROPE 1944

GREAT BRITAIN
NETHERLANDS
Amsterdam
GERMANY
Calais
Cherbourg
Le Havre
Antwerp
BELGIUM
St Malo
Paris
FRANCE
ITALY

→ Allied advance
➡ German counter-attack in the Ardennes

THE BATTLE OF THE BULGE

In late 1944, the Germans tried to win back the city of Antwerp in Belgium. As they pushed forward, they made the Allied lines "bulge". This gave the battle its name. But in the end the Germans were beaten.

Mussolini's death
After Italy's defeat, the people turned against their leader Mussolini and killed him in 1944.

Hand grenade

A German paratrooper fights during the Battle of the Bulge

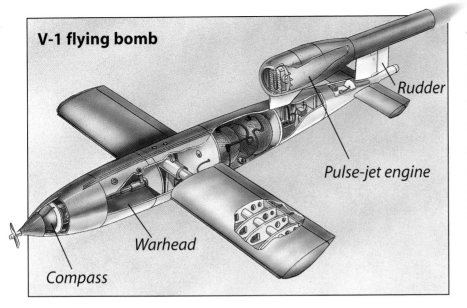

V-1 flying bomb

Rudder

Pulse-jet engine

Warhead

Compass

MADMAN IN CHARGE
By 1944, Hitler was behaving strangely. He made peculiar decisions and would not listen to advice. A group of German officers tried to kill him, but failed. They were executed (killed).

V-WEAPONS
In 1944 the Germans began to use V-1 flying bombs, which were nicknamed "doodlebugs". They were launched from France and had just enough fuel to reach London. Then they dropped to the ground and exploded. There was also a V-2 rocket bomb. Thousands of V-weapons were used against cities in Europe.

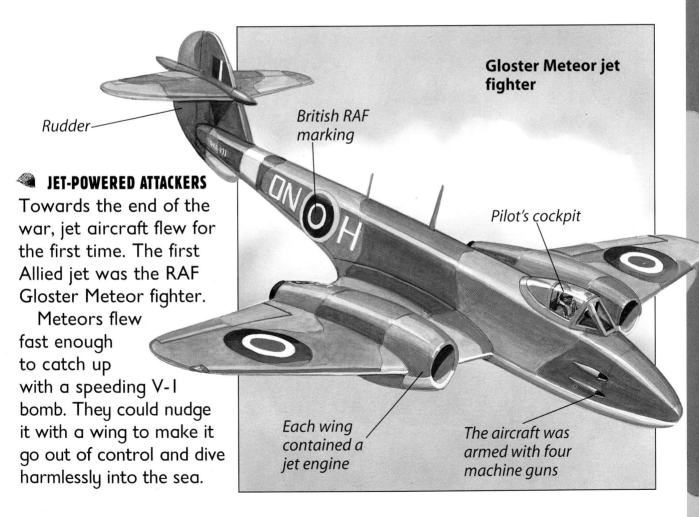

Gloster Meteor jet fighter

Rudder

British RAF marking

Pilot's cockpit

Each wing contained a jet engine

The aircraft was armed with four machine guns

JET-POWERED ATTACKERS
Towards the end of the war, jet aircraft flew for the first time. The first Allied jet was the RAF Gloster Meteor fighter.
Meteors flew fast enough to catch up with a speeding V-1 bomb. They could nudge it with a wing to make it go out of control and dive harmlessly into the sea.

THE END OF THE WAR

A Red Army soldier marches into Berlin

By the spring of 1945, German forces had collapsed. Hitler killed himself in Berlin on 30 April. The war in Europe was over and the Allies had won.

The official day of victory in Europe was 8 May 1945 (VE Day). But the war was still going in the Far East. The day of victory in Japan was 15 August 1945 (VJ Day).

Starving Jewish prisoners in a Nazi concentration camp

CONCENTRATION CAMPS

When Allied troops marched into the countries of Hitler's empire, they discovered horrific conditions in the Nazi concentration camps. Here, millions of people had been murdered in gas chambers. The camps were run by the SS on Hitler's orders. Allied soldiers rescued the prisoners who were still alive.

THE HUGE COST

Millions of people died in World War Two. For example, twenty-five million died just on the Eastern Front.

The Holocaust
Hitler hated peoples such as Jews and Gypsies, and had millions of them executed (killed). This mass murder is called the Holocaust.

BRITAIN AFTER THE WAR

Even though the war had ended, life was not easy. Thousands of families were homeless. Soldiers returning home had to get used to normal life again. The rationing of some items continued until 1954.

People in Britain held street parties to celebrate the end of the war

WAR TRIALS

The Allies put Nazis on trial for their war crimes. Those who had done terrible things were executed.

GERMANY AFTER THE WAR

At the end of the war, Germany was split into West Germany and East Germany. East Germany was under the control of the USSR until the 1990s, when East and West Germany were united and became one nation again.

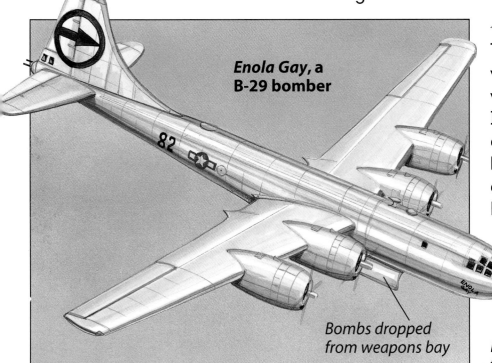

Enola Gay, a
B-29 bomber

Bombs dropped from weapons bay

FIRST NUCLEAR BOMBS

The USA used a new weapon to end the war in Japan quickly. In August 1945, it dropped nuclear bombs on the Japanese cities of Hiroshima and Nagasaki. These killed thousands of people in seconds. The Japanese had to surrender.

Enola Gay **dropped the first nuclear bomb**

GLOSSARY

Japanese soldier

Allies
The countries that fought against the Axis powers. "Allied" means "belonging to the Allies".

Axis powers
Germany, Japan, Italy and some other Eastern European countries who fought against the Allies.

Blitz
The nightly bombing of British cities during 1940–41.

Blitzkrieg
The German army's fast advance through Europe in 1939–40.

British RAF pilot

Campaign
The period of time when an army is fighting an enemy.

Concentration camps
Brutal prisons set up by the Nazis to wipe out people they hated.

Conquer
To defeat and take over (for example an army or a country).

Convoy
A group of merchant ships guarded by armed ships.

Counter-attack
An attack made in response to an attack.

D-Day
When the Allies landed in France on 6 June 1944 to begin freeing Europe from Nazi occupation.

Defeat
To beat someone in a battle or war.

Dictator
A leader who makes everyone do as he says.

Fleet
A number of warships.

Gestapo
The Nazi secret police.

GIs
A nickname for ordinary American soldiers.

Holocaust
The murder of millions of Jews and other peoples by the Nazi SS.

Hitler, Adolf
Adolf Hitler was the dictator of Germany

and leader of the Nazi Party. He was also known as the Führer.

Invade
To go into another country or its land using armed forces.

Luftwaffe
The German air force.

Merchant shipping
Ships that carried food and goods from one country to another.

Military
Something that is to do with the armed forces.

Minesweeper
A ship that finds and destroys explosive underwater mines.

Nazi
A member of Hitler's National Socialist party.

Neutral country
A country that says it will not join in with a war.

Occupied countries
The countries that Germany marched into and took over.

Patrol
To move around an area to make sure it is safe.

RADAR
A detection system that bounces radio waves against a distant object to find where it is.

RAF
British Royal Air Force.

Red Army
The army of the Communist USSR.

Resistance
People in an occupied country who secretly fight their conquerors.

Australian soldier

Sabotage
Secretly destroying, damaging and disrupting things.

SS
Nazi military police.

Tactics
Special plans that an army makes to try and win in battle.

U-boat
German submarine.

USSR
The Union of Soviet Socialist Republics, often referred to as "Russia".

Wolfpack
A group of U-boats. They attacked ships.

US infantryman

INDEX

PHOTOGRAPHIC CREDITS

Hulton Getty pp. 9 (Keystone), 10 (Keystone), 15 (Keystone), 22 (Slava Katamidze/Georgi Zelma), 28 (Three Lions)
Peter Newark's Military Pictures pp. 13, 18, 25